A Chick Hatches

JOANNA COLE

photographs by

JEROME WEXLER

William Morrow and Company
New York 1976

The author would like to thank
Daniel W. Talmadge, Associate Professor,
Department of Poultry Science
at the University of Connecticut
for his helpful reading of the manuscript

Library of Congress Cataloging in Publication Data

Cole, Joanna.
    A chick hatches.

    SUMMARY: Photographic presentation of what happens
inside the chicken egg during its twenty-one day incubation period.
    1.Chick embryo—Juvenile literature. [1.Chick embryo.
2.Reproduction. 3.Eggs] I.Wexler, Jerome. II.Title.
QL959.C56   598.6'1   76-29017
ISBN 0-688-22087-8
ISBN 0-688-32087-2 lib. bdg.

What is inside this egg?
Do you know?

Crack open the shell.
You can see the yellow yolk
and the clear white of the egg,
which is called the "albumen."

Sticking to the inside of the shell
is a thin white skin
called the "shell membrane."

In the large end of the egg,
there is an air space.

Air comes into the space
through tiny holes, or pores, in the shell.

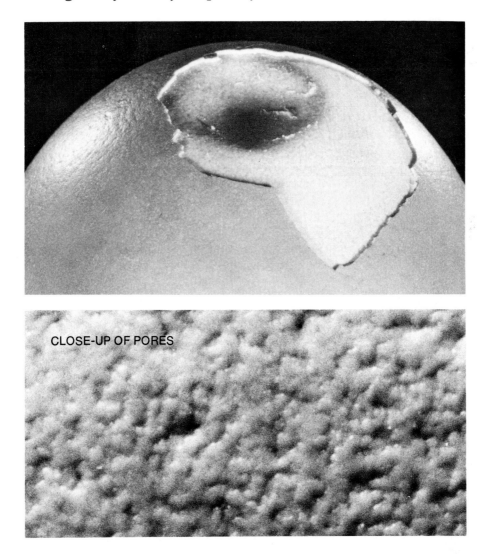

CLOSE-UP OF PORES

There is something else in the egg too.
It is this white spot on the yolk.
Before the egg was laid,
the hen mated with a rooster.
The rooster's sperm
joined with the ovum cell on the yolk.
Inside the hen's body,
that single cell grew into hundreds of cells.
This white spot is the beginning of a chick.

If the egg is kept warm
for twenty-one days—or three weeks—
a chick will hatch.

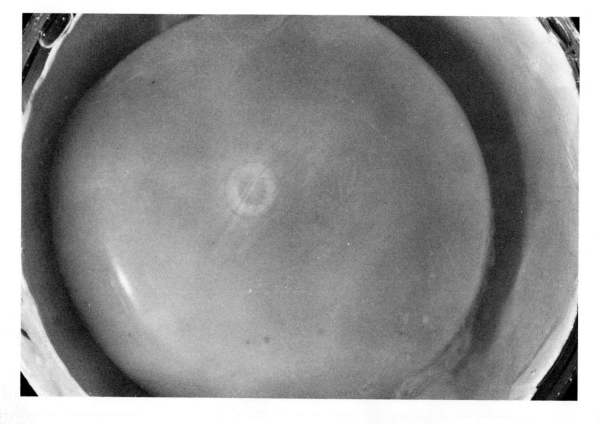

The eggs that we buy for eating
were laid by hens
that did not mate with a rooster.

These eggs have a white spot too,
but it is very small.
It cannot grow into a chick.

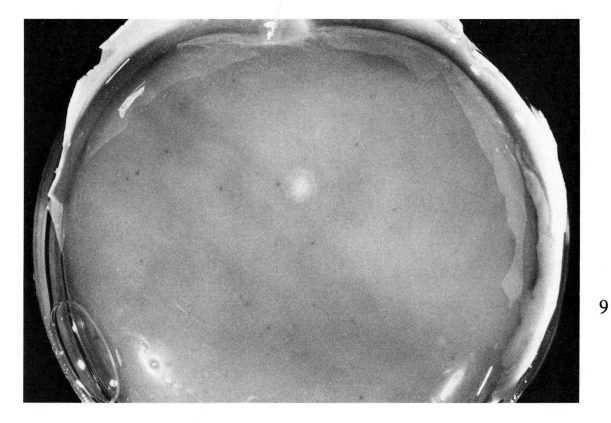

In order to grow,
the white spot needs warmth,
which it gets from the hen's body
or from an incubator.
It needs food and water,
which it gets from the yolk.
And it needs oxygen,
which it gets from the air
that comes in through the shell's air holes.

After the egg has been kept warm
for twenty-four hours,
the white spot has grown much larger.

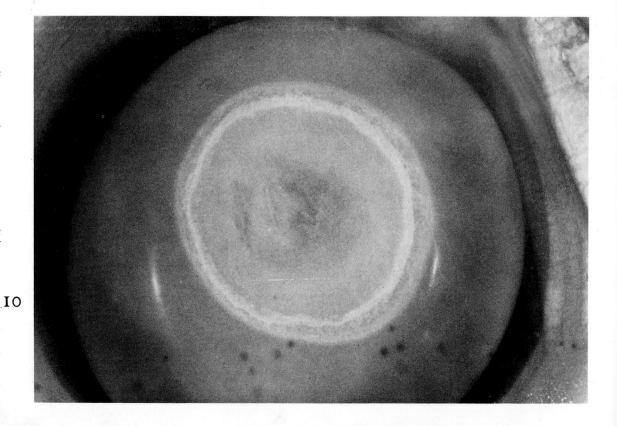

It started out as a single cell
inside the hen's body.
By the time the egg was laid,
it had grown to several hundred cells.
Now it is several thousand cells.

After two days the white spot has changed.
The cells are forming
what will be the chick's body.
Now the spot is called an "embryo."

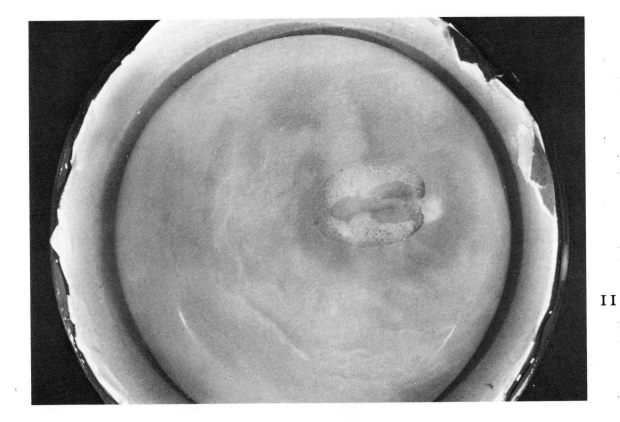

The top of the embryo
will be the chick's head.
The bottom will be its tail.
The dark grains
are the beginnings of blood vessels.

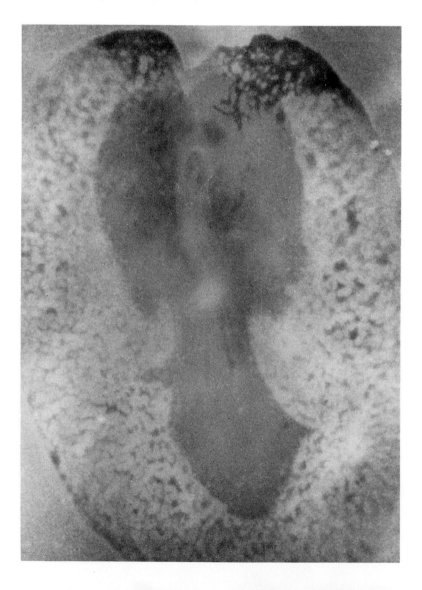

By the third day,
the embryo has grown
into the shape of a backwards question mark.
The top part of the question mark is the head.

The dark spot in the middle is the heart.
It is actually beating!

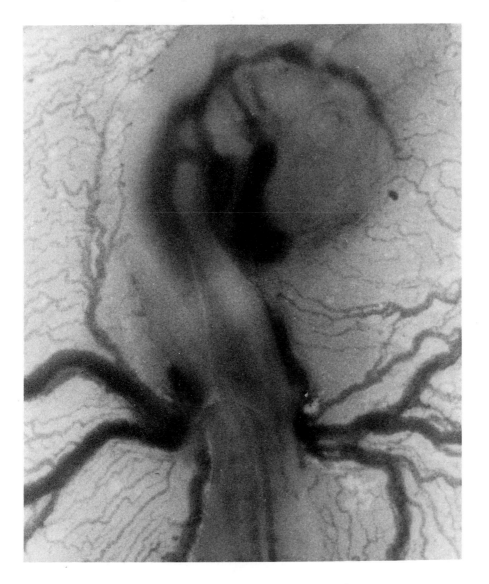

A network of blood vessels
stretches over the surface of the yolk.

The heart pumps the blood through the vessels.
The blood comes back to the embryo,
bringing food and water from the yolk.
In this way the embryo is nourished.

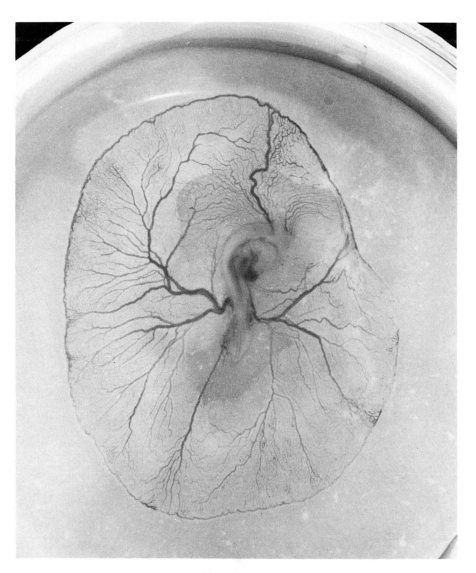

After four days you can see the eye—
the dark, round spot on the head.
The embryo is growing fast and needs more food.
To bring this food from the yolk,
more and more blood vessels have formed.

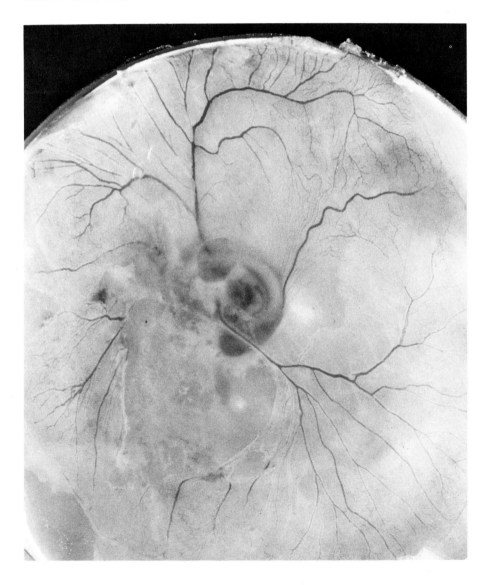

A clear pouch, called the "amniotic sac,"
has grown around the embryo.
Inside the sac,
the embryo moves about in a watery fluid.

The amniotic sac protects the embryo
and gives it a safe place to develop.

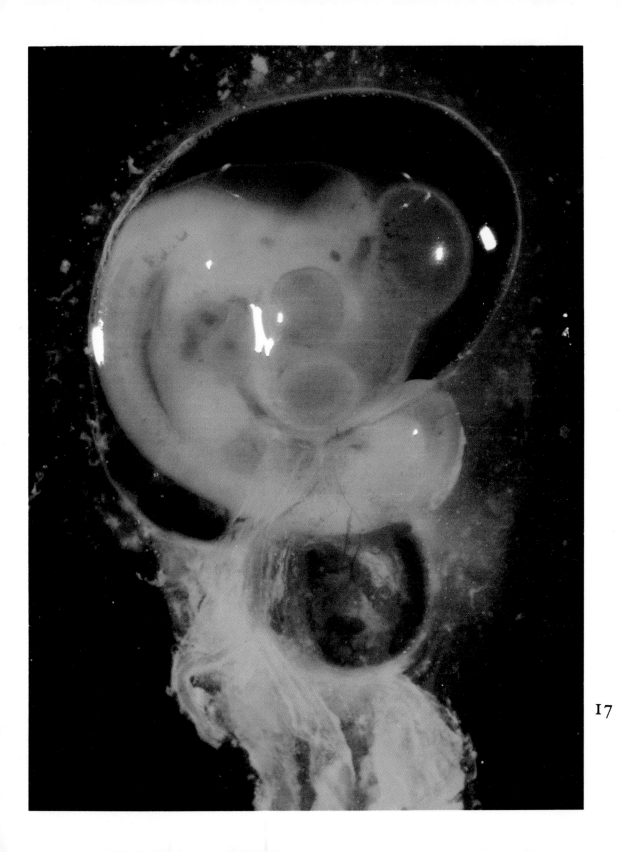

17

By the fifth day,
the embryo has changed even more.
As the chick floats in the amniotic sac,
you can see the little buds
that will become its wings and legs.

Another sac is growing.
This one is called
the "allantois (al' lan-twas) membrane."
It looks like a shadow in the picture.

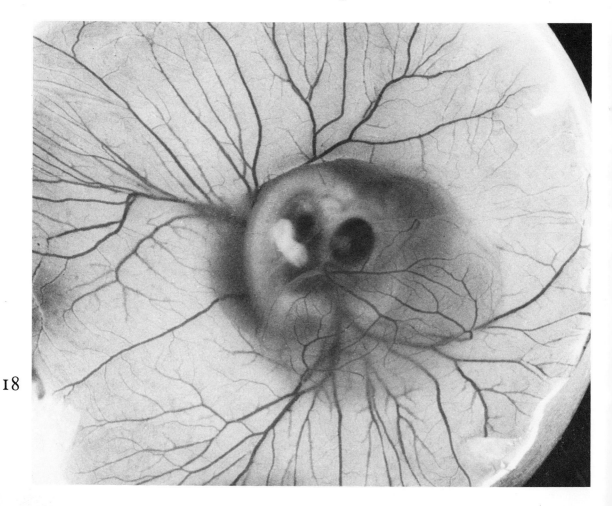

The allantois is full of blood vessels
that take in oxygen from the air.
The blood carries the oxygen to the embryo.
And it carries away carbon dioxide.
In this way the embryo "breathes,"
even though it is completely submerged
in the watery fluid inside the amniotic sac.

In time, the allantois will grow all around
the yolk, the albumen, and the embryo.

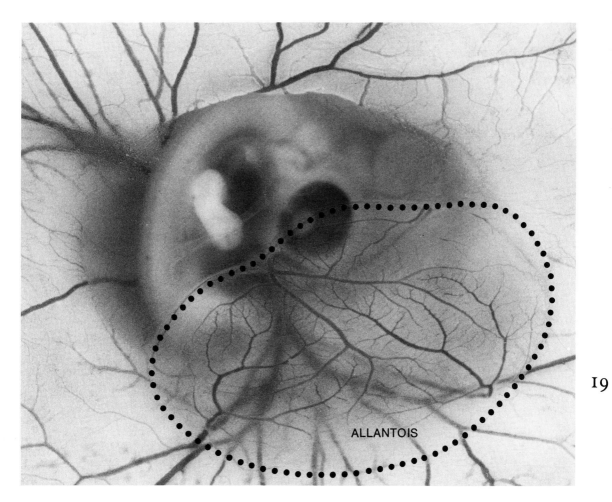

ALLANTOIS

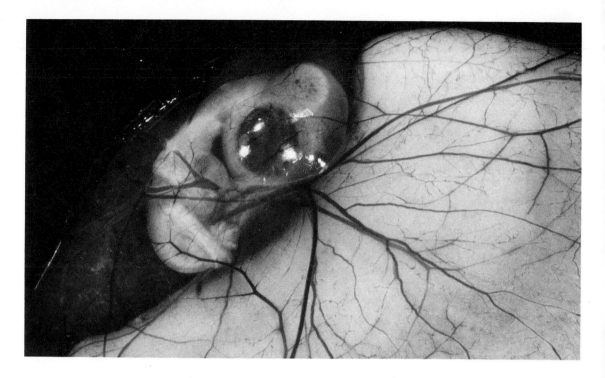

The embryo has been kept warm
for one week now,
and it has reached a new stage.
From now on it is called a "fetus."

The fetus has all the parts
that the finished chick will have.
It has the beginnings
of a brain, a heart, and a stomach.
It has eyes, ears, and a beak.
Even its toes are all there.
They are not developed,
but they are started.

This picture clearly shows
the world of the fetus inside the egg.

The fetus floats inside the amniotic sac
and is attached to the yolk
by a stalk of blood vessels.
Notice how the network of blood vessels
is growing around the yolk.
The albumen, or clear white of the egg,
is seen at the right.

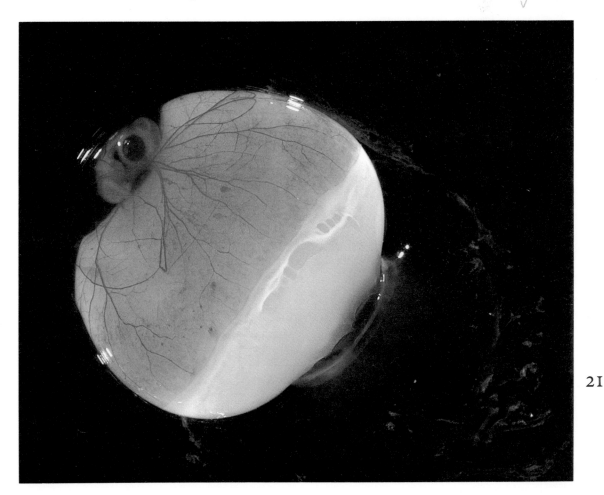

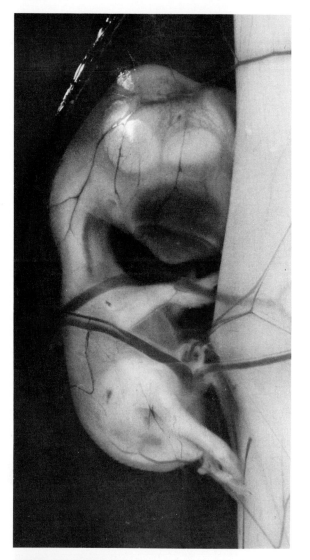

By the eighth day,
the fetus is larger.
The legs and wings
are better developed.

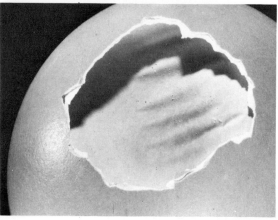

The air space
in the large end of the egg
is bigger too.

22

At nine days
the fetus is starting to look like a chick.
The beak is formed.
The wings are shaped like a chicken's wings.
Even the little stump of a tail is there.

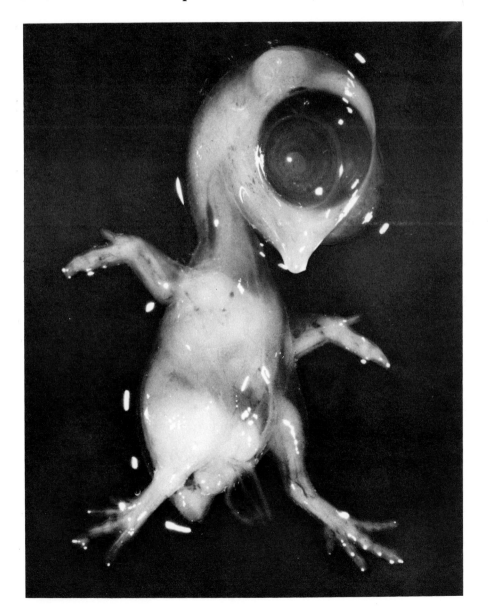

Two days later, at eleven days,
the eyelids are formed.
The beak opens and closes.
The "goose bumps" on the skin
are the beginnings of feathers.

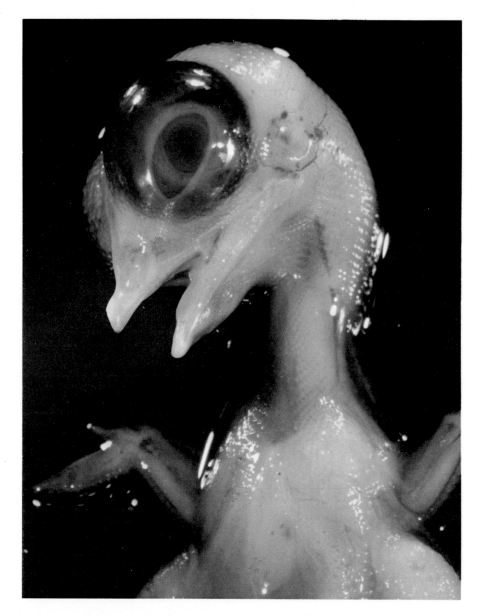

When the fetus is two weeks old,
it has feathers on its body
and claws on its toes.
It is a lot bigger too.

Before long things are crowded inside the egg.

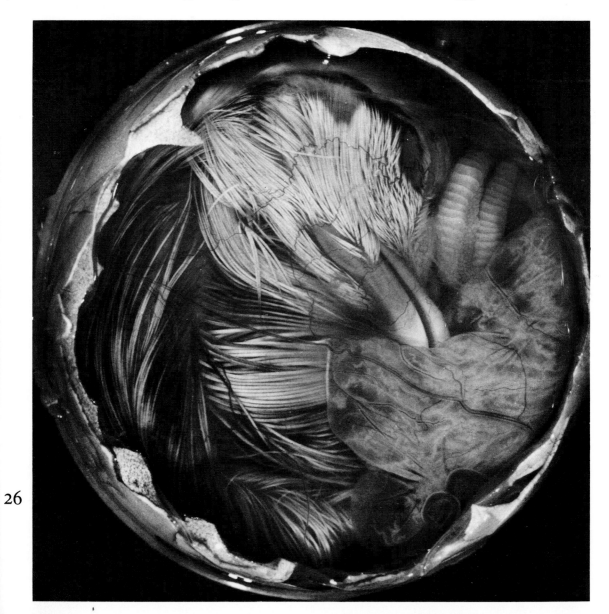

The allantois membrane,
which carries the oxygen,
has grown all around the fetus.

Besides helping the chick breathe,
the allantois takes in calcium from the shell
to help form the chick's bones.

It also acts as a "garbage pail."
The stringy white material is waste matter,
which will be stored in the allantois
until the chick hatches.

Inside the membrane,
the fetus looks more and more like a chick.

Notice how much of the yolk has been used up.
Every day now until hatching
some of the yolk will be drawn into the chick's body.

By the eighteenth day,
half the remaining yolk
has been used as food.

By the nineteenth day,
there is only a little bit left.
Right before hatching,
it too will be drawn into the chick's body.

After hatching, the chick will not need
to eat or drink for a few days.
The last bit of yolk will provide nourishment.

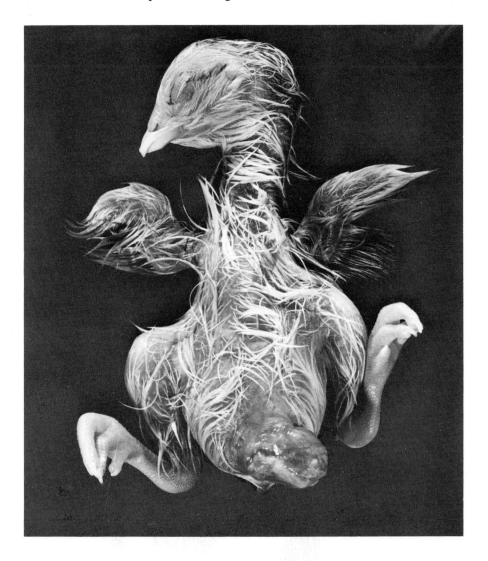

The day before hatching,
the chick pokes a hole in the sac.
It sticks its head through the shell membrane
into the air space
and takes a breath.

The chick is still getting oxygen
through the blood vessels,
but it has to practice breathing before it hatches.
Then it will be able to get oxygen
as soon as it breaks out of the shell.

Once its head is in the air space,
you can hear the chick peeping loudly
inside the shell!

On the chick's beak,
you can see the egg tooth.
This tooth is a sharp little bump
that will help the chick break the shell.
A few days after hatching,
the egg tooth will drop off.

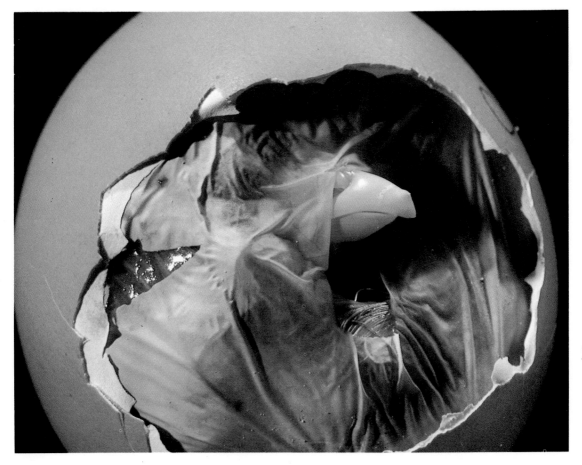

On the twenty-first day—
three weeks after the egg was first laid
with its little white spot—
the chick pecks a small hole in the shell.
The pecking is hard work.
After the hole is made,
the chick seems to go to sleep.
Nothing more is heard from it for hours.

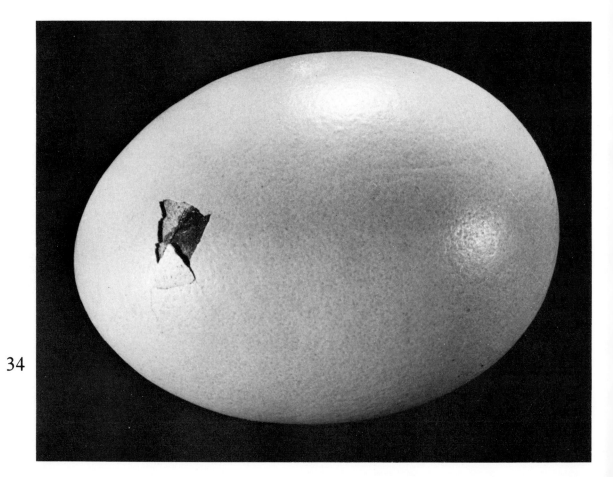

Then all at once,
the chick is pecking again, fast and furiously.
As it breaks the shell,
the chick turns around inside.
Watch the little circle drawn on the eggshell
in the next pictures.
You can see how the egg rolls over
as the chick pecks.

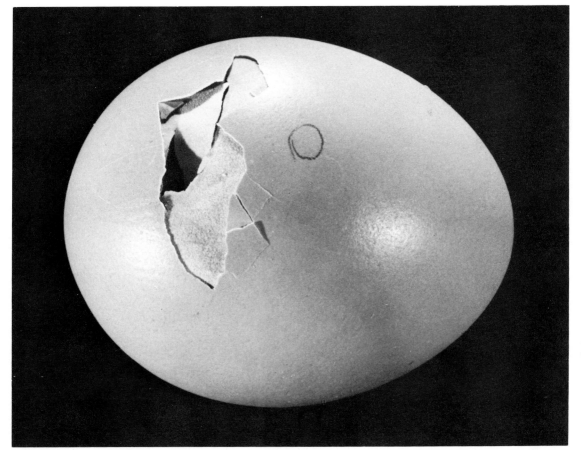

Peck...

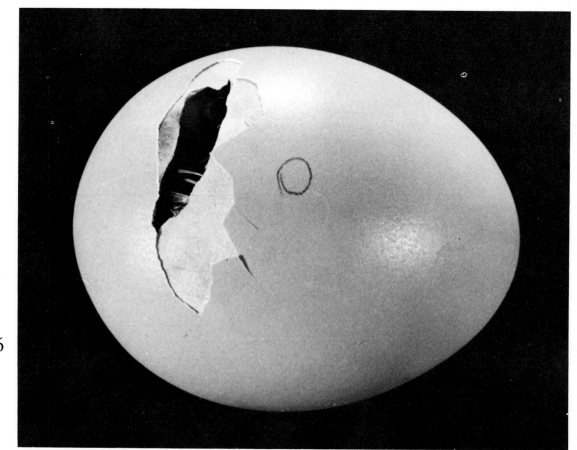

36

peck...

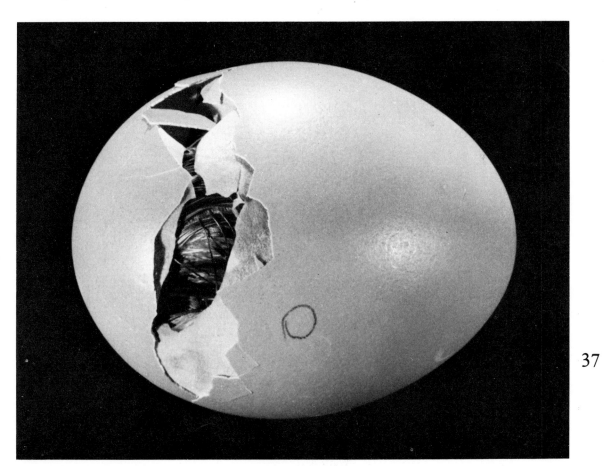

peck!

Now the shell is broken
almost all the way around.

The chick gives a mighty kick
with its big feet and. . .

bursts out of the shell!

What a sight!
The chick is wet and tired.
It flops on its stomach and rests.

The last little bit of yolk
has been drawn into its body.

Left behind in the shell
is the allantois membrane
with the waste matter.

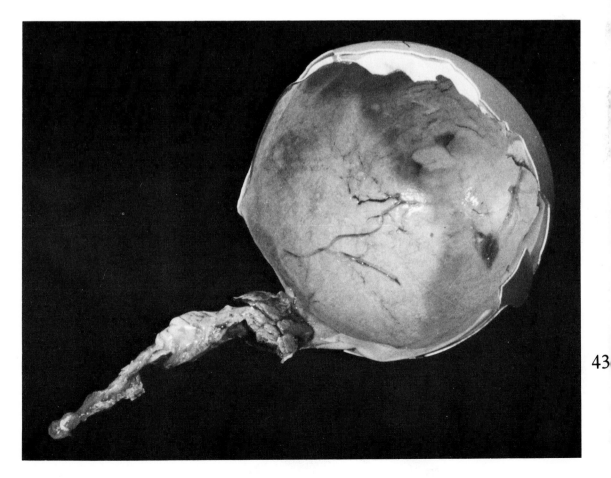

The chick tries to walk, but it is too weak.
It hobbles about, using its wings as props.

Bits of fluff float around
as the chick's feathers dry.

Two days after hatching,
the chick is on its own.
But it is not finished growing yet.
It will get much bigger.
Its downy feathers will be replaced
by larger ones.

In about six months,
this baby chick will be a full-grown chicken.

47

Born in Newark, New Jersey, Joanna Cole grew up in East Orange.
After attending the University of Massachusetts
and Indiana University, she earned a B.A. degree in psychology
at the City College of New York. Later she took graduate courses
in elementary education at New York University
and served for one year in a Brooklyn elementary school as a librarian.
Mrs. Cole now is a children's book editor.
She and her husband live in New York City.

Jerome Wexler was born in New York City, where he attended
Pratt Institute. Later he studied at the University of Connecticut.
His interest in photography started when he was in the ninth grade.
After service in World War II, he worked for the State Department
in Europe as a photographer. Returning to the United States,
he specialized in photographing advanced farming techniques,
and the pictures he made have been published throughout the world.
   Now chief photographer for *Visual Teaching,* an audiovisual company
specializing in slide sets and filmstrips for use in schools,
Mr. Wexler lives in Wallingford, Connecticut.

DATE DUE

DEC 1 6 1997			

THE LIBRARY STORE   #47-0103 Pre-Gummed